7/04

P9-CDS-677

What's Inside a Police Station?

Sharon Gordon

BENCHMARK BOOKS

MARSHALL CAVENDISH
NEW YORK

Inside a Police Station

1 chief's office   3 dispatch center

2 computer room   4 front desk

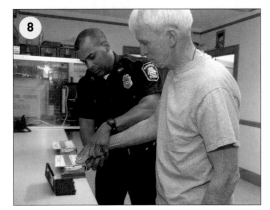

5 jail cell

6 police dog

7 police lab

8 processing room

Welcome to the police station.
Police officers start their day here.

There are many offices inside the police station. The *chief of police* has his own office. He is in charge of the police station. He plans the day's work for the police officers.

A dispatch center is inside the police station. The *dispatcher* takes emergency calls. She tells the officers what happened and where to go.

In the computer room, officers can get maps and directions. They can also find information about drivers and cars. The officers can check to see if a car has been stolen.

People with all kinds of problems come to the front desk. Some come to complain about a noisy neighbor. Others have lost something important. The officers know how to help.

Some police stations have a harbor patrol. The harbor patrol looks for people who break the law in boats.

Police boats also help rescue people who have had an accident on the water.

Police officers try to catch people who have broken laws. Breaking the law is called a *crime*.

A person who breaks the law is a *criminal*. When the police arrest him, he is taken to the police station.

Inside the station, the officers
ask the *suspect* questions and
write a report.

They keep their reports in a file
so other officers can read them.

The police officers may charge the suspect with a crime. He might have to stay overnight in the jail cell.

In the *processing room,* an officer takes the suspect's *fingerprints* with an inkpad. He presses them onto special fingerprint cards.

The fingerprints are kept with a photograph of the criminal. This will help the officers find him in the future.

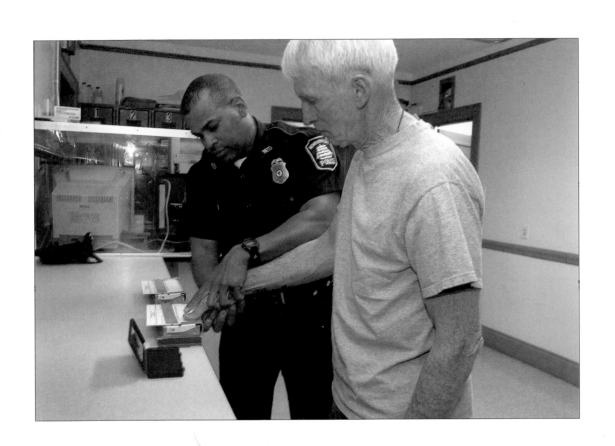

Sometimes the officers need help solving a crime. They call in the detectives.

A *detective* does not wear a police uniform. She looks like everyone else on the street.

The detective questions the suspect. She looks for *evidence*, or clues, such as a piece of hair or clothing.

The evidence is sent to the police lab. The workers in the lab study it to find out what happened.

The police dog is trained to track down clues. He can help the officers find people and objects.

The police dog is always ready to get to work!

Challenge Words

chief of police—The officer in charge of the police station.

crime—An action that is against the law.

criminal—A person who breaks the law.

detective—A police officer who works to solve crimes.

dispatcher—A phone operator who takes emergency calls for the police, ambulance, and fire stations.

evidence (e-vuh-dents)—Clues about a crime.

fingerprints—Marks made when the fingertips are pressed in ink and then onto paper.

processing room (prah-ses-ing room)—A room inside the police station where fingerprints are made.

suspect—A person who may have broken the law.

Index

Page numbers in **boldface** are illustrations.

With thanks to Nanci Vargus, Ed.D.
and Beth Walker Gambro, reading consultants

ACKNOWLEDGMENTS
With thanks to the Amesbury, Massachusetts, Police Department
and the Newburyport, Massachusetts, Police Department

Benchmark Books
Marshall Cavendish
99 White Plains Road
Tarrytown, New York 10591-9001
www.marshallcavendish.com

Library of Congress Cataloging-in-Publication Data

Gordon, Sharon.
What's inside a police station? / by Sharon Gordon.
p. cm. — (Bookworms: What's inside?)
Includes index.
Summary: An introduction to life at a police department, including
descriptions of the equipment, the staff, and what happens on a typical day.
ISBN 0-7614-1566-1
1. Police—Juvenile literature. 2. Police stations—Juvenile
literature. 3. Police—Equipment and supplies—Juvenile literature.
[1. Police. 2. Police stations.] I. Title. II. Series: Gordon, Sharon.
Bookworms. What's inside?

HV7922.G66 2003
363.2—dc21
2003005160

Photo Research by Anne Burns Images

Cover Photo by Jay Mallin
All of the photographs used in this book were taken by and used with the permission of Jay Mallin.

Series design by Becky Terhune

Printed in China
1   3   5   6   4   2